50 WINNING LESSONS

in
Business
and
Life

James A. Kimble

Copyright © 2024 James A. Kimble
All rights reserved
First Edition

PAGE PUBLISHING
Conneaut Lake, PA

First originally published by Page Publishing 2024

ISBN 979-8-89315-149-7 (pbk)
ISBN 979-8-89315-163-3 (digital)

Printed in the United States of America

Disclaimer

This book is designed to provide accurate and authoritative information about the subject matter covered. However, the author and publisher make no representations or warranties with respect to the accuracy or completeness of the contents of this book, and they specifically disclaim any liability, loss, or risk, personal or otherwise, which is incurred as a consequence, directly or indirectly, of the use/application of the advice and strategies contained herein.

No part of this publication may be reproduced, stored in a retrieval system, or transmitted in any form or by any means, electronic, mechanical, photocopying, recording, scanning, or otherwise, except as permitted under Section 107 or 108 of the 1976 US copyright act.

Praise

"Jim is the consummate professional with high business integrity, extensive industry knowledge, and brings great insights into his engagements around innovation, trends and creating new business growth with his ability to build meaningful relationships and partnerships."

—R&D executive

"Jim is one of the brightest, most professional, detailed, thoughtful, honest and fun people to work with. He has been instrumental in leading the company to pursue directions with results of the greatest magnitude; he was tremendous at navigating challenging circumstances to always inform corporate leadership of what they needed to hear, not necessarily what they wanted to hear. Jim is a developer of ideas and pathways to accomplishment. He is a person one seeks out when endeavoring to improve and advance your strategic initiatives."

—CEO and President

"Jim is extremely astute and able to quickly assess the opportunity or problem and offer outstanding solutions. He is very professional and easy to work with."

—Key customer

"Jim brings a passion to business development and to the people within the business. He offers a visionary prospective to business."

—HR and Procurement colleague

"Jim has a great understanding of how to put deals together that benefit both parties and manages the process with great expertise. He is very creative in his out of the box thinking and approach to situations. He is also very open to the ongoing relationships after deals are signed and ensures that things work out for the long term for everyone. He knows how to manage the business ensuring success for all parties."

—Alliance colleague

Contents

Introduction — ix-x

50 Winning Lessons — 1-61

Bonus Lessons — 62-68

Closing — 69

Introduction

*"Every moment I shape my destiny with a chisel.
I am a carpenter of my own soul."*
—Marcus Aurelius

This book was written for three reasons.

First, having recently retired from 40 years in business, I needed a new project that I could embrace and turn my passion into. My wife of over 25 years, Bonnie, knew too well that I could not sit idly around. It was in both of our best interests to have something to dedicate myself to. Thanks, Bonnie!

Second, since my retirement, I have had numerous requests from former business colleagues to continue to provide business assistance in some manner. I was searching for the right work-life balance, as the primary reason for my retirement was to reduce daily work stress. Unfortunately, shortly after my retirement, I had a bad bicycling fall that severely broke my right clavicle. During my recovery, my activities were very limited, so I read a lot of books (almost one per day). Fortunately, one of the books I had the opportunity to read was by a former CEO of mine, David R. Lumley. His book, *It's Impossible to Commit to Maybe,* gave me the inspiration to write my own book as the answer to the next adventure. Thanks, Dave!

Third, on a visit back to Sedona, Arizona, for our 25th wedding anniversary, my wife and I met up with some good friends. One of my retired friends told me one of the challenges he had found with retirement. He said that it was a shame not to utilize and share the unique skill set that he had built up over his career and life. That hit home to me and is what I will try to do with this book. Hopefully, you can put some of this to good use in your own life and career. Thanks, Jerry!

The book is based on applied learning from my life and business career.

One of my strengths is observing and processing a large amount of data and experiences, cherry-picking key learnings, and communicating them in an understandable manner with comparisons to life experiences where applicable. This went back to the way I was raised and my competitive family, sports, academics, and life experiences. Thanks to my family, coaches, teammates, teachers, colleagues, and friends!

The approach here, as opposed to other books, is to try to provide a much simpler tool to learn and to use for business and life. You will learn the power and benefit of a one-page summary and the negative impact of 300-page documents with expensive consultants.

These lessons are succinctly summarized with examples and stories that can be applied individually and more powerfully combined together to help you win in business and life.

For an extended version of this book that also includes practical, real-world examples in **S**trategy, **O**rganic growth and acquisitions, **A**sset management, and **R**ewards/results assessment, please read the book *WINNING: Simple, Effective, Lessons/Framework to SOAR*.

For a complementary book that provides practical lessons, examples, and case studies in **S**trategy, **O**rganic growth and acquisitions, **A**sset management, and **R**ewards/results assessment, please read *SOAR to WIN*.

Enjoy and I hope this helps you win more in business and life, however that is defined for you!

50 Winning Lessons

"If you could erase all the mistakes of your past, you would erase the wisdom of your present. Remember the lesson, not the disappointment."
—Unknown

Preface

"If you don't know where you are going, any road will take you there."
—Lewis Carroll

To capture and leverage the wisdom of your present and win in the future, develop and follow your strategic plan in business and life.

The strategic plan should be simple and tailored to you.

It needs to include and focus on your few, most important priorities.

It should incorporate the **50 Winning Lessons** that follow.

Once you have developed your strategic plan, you need to consistently use it as your overarching guidebook. It is not meant to be a strict checklist for your daily activities; rather, it should be a beacon to keep you on course over your long journey ahead.

Develop and follow your strategic plan to know where you are going. Your road will then take you there.

50 Winning Lessons

1. Commit to Your Passion 7
2. Define Winning 9
3. Clarify Your Target Market 11
4. Identify Key Drivers/Differentiators 12
5. Define and Live Your Brand 13
6. Do the Right Things 14
7. Prioritize 17
8. Simplify 18
9. Less Is More 19
10. 10/50, 20/80, 30/90 20
11. Focus 21
12. Align 22
13. Define/Develop Clear Roles/Skill Sets 23
14. Instill Responsibility/Accountability 24
15. Build Winning Values/Culture 25
16. Hire/Retain/Promote/Reward Values Fit 26
17. Hire/Leverage/Align Strengths 27
18. Reward/Reinforce Desired Performance 28
19. Set High Standards 29
20. Do Things Right 30
21. Employ Winning Habits 31
22. Use RFP 32
23. Deploy an A+ Virtual Team 33
24. Cultivate Relationships 34
25. Actions Over Words 35

50 Winning Lessons

26. Silence Is Power..36
27. Remove Cancer Early 37
28. Innovate..38
29. Define the Root Issue...39
30. Depth before Breadth 40
31. Protect Core Profits..41
32. Cash Is King...42
33. Embrace Reality...43
34. Openly Debate, Then Align 44
35. Illusory Precision 45
36. Common Sense Wins 46
37. Use All of Your Senses.......................................47
38. Learn from History/Others.................................48
39. Understand Many Perspectives..........................50
40. Engage Your Stakeholders 51
41. Coach/Teach, Don't Manage..............................52
42. Minimize Inward Activity..................................53
43. Minimize Presentations......................................54
44. Walking around Works.......................................55
45. No Annual Budget..56
46. Take Annual Physical...57
47. Do Scenario/Contingency Planning 58
48. Play Chess..59
49. Celebrate True Wins...60
50. Use One-Page Summaries..................................61

Lesson 1
Commit to Your Passion

"It's not the years in your life that count, it's the life in your years."
—Abraham Lincoln

Your life and career have a limited time horizon. This is becoming more evident to me as I have recently retired and my health has started to restrict my leisure capabilities.

This is why Lesson 1 is to Commit to Your Passion. It is the most important lesson, as it is something few people and businesses truly do.

Everyone has a unique passion that drives them. It only makes sense to spend most of your time fueling it. This is true for you and for your business. It is well understood by highly successful competitors and entrepreneurs. Unfortunately, most go through life working on tasks that take them away from their happiness and success.

Different textbooks and companies use a variety of terminology to describe this. Some call it *purpose*. Some call it *mission statement*. I prefer to call it *passion*, as it has more meaning and impact if there is a strong emotional connection to it beyond just words.

Your passion should specifically answer two questions: what and why.
What activity are you most emotionally connected to?
Why is there this emotional connection?

My passion in my career was to work on strategy and acquisitions. I was given a great opportunity early in my career at a major company to recommend the optimal strategic business portfolio. I fell in love with this, as the impact of the decision was legacy-altering for the company. More in Lesson 6, "Do the Right Things." A few years later, I had an opportunity with acquisitions at a consumer products firm that had a similar impact.

My personal life passion was spending my free time in the West/Southwest USA, enjoying the great outdoors. I went to a friend's wedding in Colorado in the 80s and immediately felt connected to the area. I made numerous visits to the West/Southwest, increasingly often since then, and finally moved to Arizona full-time in 2019.

Many businesses make the mistake of creating a purpose or mission statement that is too general or vague. The statement could apply to numerous companies and often lacks an emotional connection. As a result, it does not provide the required rallying cry and inspiration to effectively lead the business to win against tough competition. Don't do this. Make yours specific and tailored to you.

Once you identify your passion, the next step is to truly commit to it.
This means the majority of your resources and time should be spent on it, not on the vast number of competing tasks that take away from it.

To do this, follow the remaining Winning Lessons in this book.

Lesson 2
Define Winning

"The person you are destined to become is the person you decide to be."
—Ralph Waldo Emerson

To know if you are winning, you must first define what it means to you. Every individual and company has different definitions of what this is.

This is easier to define in sports. For a game, winning is determined by the score at the end of the game or event. Each game generally has a winner. Each season, there is one champion. But even in sports, competitors and teams will have different definitions of what winning means. For a highly successful team or individual, winning may mean being crowned a champion. For others, it could mean finishing a marathon for the first time, qualifying for an event, having a personal or franchise-best result, or even just competing.

Winning in life is highly individualized. Each person has a different definition and a unique passion. For someone to be truly happy, they need to determine what winning means to them, not what winning means to others (neighbors, friends, peer pressure standards, etc.). For some, it can be money, although this is, generally, not what makes most people happy. For some, it can be finding your soulmate and raising a family. For others, it can be achieving your passion or making a lasting difference in society. There is no correct answer here for all—it must be tailored to the person.

My personal definition of winning is shaped by my upbringing and life experiences. I am from a large family with eight kids and grew up in Green Bay, Wisconsin. This led me to be highly competitive and sports-focused. I was primarily raised by my mother, as my father passed away when I was nine. My mother set very high expectations for us and was a tremendous role model. This combination drove me to competitively excel in academics and sports that I played—I always needed to make my best effort to win where possible. But it was not about winning at all costs.

I was brought up with strong values that you needed to do it the right way and with the right balance.

Winning in my career was not defined by dollars. Sure, I wanted to achieve and be financially rewarded, but I didn't need to maximize my salary. I had the opportunity to move into the highly lucrative investment banking field. It would have required me to move to NYC and work around the clock. These trade-offs were not worth it to me as I valued a better work-life balance, and they were not consistent with my passion as described in Lesson 1.

Winning in my life was defined by finding the right soulmate and following my passion. I have been extremely fortunate to do both. I finally met my soulmate at the age of 36, and we have been happily married for over 25 years now. More on this story in Bonus Lesson 4, "Sometimes the Best Decisions Are Ones Not Made."

Winning in business is also customized. No two businesses share the same standard of what winning means. You may have competitors who are vying to be number 1 in their particular industry segment, but they will have different definitions of winning. Stakeholders (shareholders/owners, investors/partners, employees, customers, suppliers, and the community) in each business will vary, and this will necessarily impact what winning means. Many companies chase scale because they mistakenly believe that size defines winning. Size may be one of the metrics in a balanced scorecard, but often it is not truly how stakeholders define winning. It can also lead to harmful resource allocation.

Your definition of winning may also change over time and with changes in your life or business situation. If it does, make the necessary adjustment.

Spend time to clearly define what winning means to you.
You will be happier and more successful as a result.

Lesson 3
Clarify Your Target Market

"Everyone is not your customer."

—Seth Godin

One cannot effectively serve everyone, everywhere, all the time. So it is critical to determine what your target market is.

To do this, you need to answer three questions: who, where, and when.

Who is my target customer? Families? Trail runners? College students? Retirees? Cat owners? The possibilities are endless. The more specific segments with clear needs that you identify, the easier it is to tailor the solution to fit them and the easier it is to differentiate yourself.

Where is my target segment? Is it local, regional, countrywide, or global?

When will I sell my product/service? 24/7? 9–5 weekdays? June–August?

It is equally important to answer three additional questions. Choices must be made to win.

Who is not my target customer?
Where won't I sell my product or invest my time and resources?
When won't I sell it?

This concept can also be applied to your life. Personally, I used this to help determine what industries and companies I would and would not work for. My target career market was a technology-led, consumer-product business with culture and leadership aligned to my values and with products I believed in and could recommend to my friends. I had the good fortune of working in my target markets for most of my career and turned down many opportunities in industries that were against my values.

Clarify your target market. Stay disciplined. Serve them well. Win.

Lesson 4
Identify Key Drivers/Differentiators

"In differentiation, not in uniformity, lies the path of progress."
—Louis D. Brandeis

Winning businesses, sports teams, and individuals typically have a few key drivers that truly differentiate themselves from the competition. They understand these and continually focus their resources to build upon and communicate them. The most powerful combine the key drivers together to create a much stronger, more defensible advantage.

When starting out, identify a list of key drivers that will have the biggest impact on your target market. The list needs to be short and prioritized. More on this in Lessons 7, "Prioritize," and 8, "Simplify."

After you are established, keep these key drivers top of mind and continually build and defend them. If you acquire a business, make sure you truly understand what their key success drivers are and absolutely protect them after integration.

The biggest driver of business performance is the quality of its products and services relative to those of its competitors. Other key drivers include real market growth, market position, investment intensity, and innovation.

One stellar example of Lesson 4 is Tesla. When they entered the electric vehicle market, the key competitors' value driver was that the vehicle was electric. Tesla disrupted the entire market by focusing its value drivers on performance and design while also being electric. They combined all three together and became the clear premium alternative fuel vehicle.

Focus on your key profitability and growth drivers. Soar.

Lesson 5
Define and Live Your Brand

"Your brand is what people say about you when you're not in the room"
—Jeff Bezos

Each person and business has a brand, whether formalized or not.

Brands are both extremely powerful and fragile at the same time.

They need to be carefully selected, cultivated, and built, then absolutely protected at all times. Brands are a lot like your trust and honor—they take a lot of time and effort to build and one moment to lose. This fact is becoming painfully obvious to many brands (Fox News, Bud Light, Target, Disney, Boeing, Harvard) today with the lightning speed of social media and product boycotts.

Your brand is your most valuable asset and needs to be treated and managed that way.

To select the right brand for you, please use Lessons 1 to 4 as your starting point. Your brand should describe and speak to your unique passion, definition of winning, core target market, and key differentiators.

My brand is rooted in my strong value system. I have traditional values derived from my family that stay with me today. Many of them are outlined in Lesson 15, "Build Winning Values/Culture." I have done my best to maintain this throughout my personal and work lives. This has served me well in both arenas. To do so, I passed up career advancement opportunities and business deals. I also changed companies when the culture/leadership alignment was no longer there. It was a small price to pay, as I strongly believe you need to stay true to yourself and to your brand. This holds true for companies too. It truly is a small world that is getting smaller every day.

Define and Live your Brand well. It will then be a great, powerful asset.

Lesson 6
Do the Right Things

"Do what is right, not what is easy."

—Roy T. Bennett

The importance of this lesson cannot be overstated. Understanding and following it can alter your life, career, and business legacy.

Conversely, not following this can have disastrous consequences.

Many other books teach that doing things right (Lesson 20) is more important. I disagree with this premise and will explain why below. I do agree that they are both highly important and that both are needed to win.

Two powerful business examples illustrate this.

As mentioned in Lesson 1, early in my career, I had a tremendous opportunity to assess a company's optimal business portfolio. At that time, the company's portfolio was roughly 50 percent packaged food and 50 percent restaurants. The company was outperforming most of their peers in both packaged food and in restaurants—they were doing things right. They were, however, underperforming in total compared to many of their food competitors.

After digging into this in more detail, I discovered the key reasons why. The packaged food segment was a much more attractive market segment to compete in than restaurants. Restaurants had much higher capital intensity due to the building cost and lower industry margins than packaged food. Growth in full-service restaurants was more variable as it was dependent on the health of the economy (more money in customers' wallets led to them eating out more often at higher-priced, full-service restaurants). The packaged food industry was relatively more stable.

Based on these findings, I recommended to the CEO that we exit the restaurant business and double down on the packaged food business segment. The CEO was not pleased with this recommendation. He had just set a record of consecutive quarters of EPS (earnings per share) growth and did not want any part of downsizing. After additional discussion, he did agree to hire an outside consulting firm to do their own assessment. Millions of dollars later, the outside consulting firm came to the same conclusion. The CEO was not pleased and did not present the findings to the board of directors. No change in portfolio strategy was made.

Unfortunately, the story now becomes tragic. Six months later, the company was acquired by a European firm. The first strategic move made by them was to exit the restaurant business as per the earlier recommendation. Fast forward a few years, and the remaining packaged food business was sold to a crosstown, longtime food competitor. The previously major historic food company was now just another brand in their competitor's business. Eventually, the brand would almost cease to exist entirely—a truly sad outcome for not doing the right thing.

Another powerful story is about one of the global consumer battery pioneers. This company historically led most of the global innovation and had become a major global player. Because of their successful innovation, they were selected by Polaroid to help develop a flat battery for their cameras. It was a major technological challenge. The battery company embraced the challenge and successfully created the battery required for Polaroid to be successful. They did things right.

Unfortunately, to do this, the battery company needed to allocate their top R&D and manufacturing talent to developing the new product. They also needed to invest millions and millions of dollars to build a plant for the battery. After a few years, Polaroid took the battery production in-house, and the battery company's business with this captive customer went away. That was a terrible result, but it was not the worst thing that happened.

While this battery company was investing their precious resources into this flat battery, a small company called Mallory had a different vision. Alkaline batteries were in their infancy. Most of the global competitors were dabbling in it, but it was a high-cost product and not a priority focus. Given that Mallory was a small industry player, they had less to lose and much more to gain if they could make alkaline successful. That was exactly what they did. You know them by the brand name they successfully created and built—Duracell. Again, more on that story later…

Many of the other global battery competitors saw Duracell's success and tried to follow it as quickly as they could. They were able to capture some market share, but it was not enough to catch up, given Duracell's lead and brand perception as the longest-lasting battery. However, the entire industry was disrupted. The longer-lasting alkaline batteries became the de facto standard in countries with a higher GDP. The lower-performing but less expensive zinc-carbon batteries declined materially in market volume.

Unfortunately for the global battery pioneer, they had most of their limited resources tied up with the flat battery project and were very late to respond to the market change. By the time they did, they were in a distant third place in the USA and were in financial trouble. Eventually, they sold off much of their international business and were bought and sold by several firms. They were close to bankruptcy before they were rescued by an entrepreneurial couple and rebuilt into a strong, viable company with the later help of a strong private equity owner. Nevertheless, they remained a small player in the industry.

Both the food and battery companies did things right, but they did not do the right things, and this was extremely costly.

It is not necessarily easy to determine what the right things are, but this should be the supreme focus of the company and of you individually. It is just too important not to.

You are free to choose, but you are not free from the consequences of your choice. **"Choose…Wisely"** **Do the Right Things.**

Lesson 7
Prioritize

"Your time is limited, so don't waste it living someone else's life."
—Steve Jobs

"The price of anything is the amount of life you exchange for it."
—Henry David Thoreau

The key winning step is to truly **prioritize** your life and business.

This does not mean making a long to-do list.

This does not mean making a wish list that you might do if you have time.

This does not mean ranking the items in order of how easy they are.

It needs to be very short and in order of importance, no matter how difficult the task is.

The priority list should be based on the previous six winning lessons.

You then need to truly commit to working through the priority list.

When you do this, you will win with greater frequency and be happier in life and in business.

Prioritize, then prioritize again. You will then live your best life.

Lesson 8
Simplify

"Complexity is the enemy of winning."

—Unknown

Complexity adds stress and costs to life and business at all levels. It also slows the organization down. As simplicity wins, complexity leads to more losses.

I know this too well. Complexity and stress caused me a significant health issue. While chasing my passion, we were building a house in Arizona from a long distance, while I was also working on numerous potential acquisitions. Not surprisingly, there were numerous and frequent complications in both areas that materially raised my stress. I developed atrial fibrillation (AFib) in my heart. This caused my heart rate to fluctuate wildly at times, increasing my chance of stroke. Fortunately, I caught this early enough to have successful ablation surgery, which has fixed the problem so far. More on this in Lesson 10. This also led to my recent retirement as a way to reduce my stress level.

Stress also occurs in business when you add complexity. Complexity adds material costs that increase geometrically with the addition of each SKU (stock-keeping unit). The other hidden but impactful negative impacts are that complexity reduces focus (Lesson 11) on the key priorities (Lesson 7), reduces accountability (Lesson 14), and makes it more difficult to do things right (Lesson 20). To remove complexity, question all past requirements and past methods. Design process from scratch. Ask why?

One effective simplification move was made by a former CEO of mine. During the planning process, one of his business leaders submitted a 100-page strategy document. The CEO cancelled the upcoming strategy meeting and cut off all business funding until the business leader resubmitted a prioritized, simplified 20-page plan that made true choices. That company never had this issue recur, as everyone got the message.

The winning answer is to Simplify, Simplify, Simplify.

Lesson 9
Less Is More

"Be a curator of your life. Cut things out until you're left with what you love, with what's necessary, and with what makes you happy."

—Leo Babauta

To simplify effectively, you need to do less. Yes, do less of everything, and you will find that less is actually more.

Doing less forces you to prioritize and focus on the most important items in your life and business. It gives you the time to do them well.

This is not easy to do. It is actually extremely hard. It is easier to make long lists and stay busy with a lot of activities without having to make choices or trade-offs. Unfortunately, this does not result in winning as you have defined it. You need to spend time making that hard decision on where you will allocate your precious limited resources of time and money.

Less does not mean nothing. It does mean a reasonably short, simplified, and prioritized number of activities.

Less projects and activities allow you to do the right things and do things right (Lesson 20) that truly matter to you and your business.

Less employees, customers, suppliers, stakeholders, and SKUs allow you greater Prioritization (Lesson 7), Simplicity (Lesson 8), Focus (Lesson 11), and Responsibility/Accountability (Lesson 14).

A great example of this is the legendary Vince Lombardi and the Green Bay Packers who won 5 titles from 1961–1967. In addition to creating a winning culture and expectation, Vince Lombardi simplified the offense and ran the infamous GB sweep again and again with great success.

I have often experienced the benefits of doing less and the costs of doing more in my life and career. ***Do less. Make yourself happy. Win.***

Lesson 10
10/50, 20/80, 30/90

"Strive for excellence in a few things rather than good in many." —R Koch

Many of you have heard of the 80/20 phrase and how effective it is.

I like to flip the order of that and add two important tiers.

Let's start with **10/50**. What this means is that about 10% of your customers, products/services, and SKUs generally drive 50% of your sales/profits. This represents your core customer and product base, which must always be the primary focus of your business. Never lose sight of this. Unfortunately, many companies have recently made this mistake with hugely negative impact (examples include Fox News, Bud Light, Target, Disney, and ESPN). This tier should also be given the highest product quality and service level.

The next tier is **20/80**. This means that about 20% of your customers, products/services, and SKUs generally drive 80% of your sales/profits. This is also a crucial tier, as they are valuable customers and products.

The final tier is **30/90**. This means that about 30% of your customers, products/services, and SKUs generally drive 90% of your sales/profits. This is a temporary tier. Items that fall into the lower tier need to have a plan to move up to 20/80 in a short period of time or move down and out.

The tail tier below should be eliminated. The tier adds unnecessary complexity and causes a loss of focus.

These tiers also apply to talent. Have your employees, suppliers, virtual team, and service providers in the 10/50 tier where possible, 20/80 at a minimum. When I needed my heart ablation surgery done, my wife researched and found the number 1 expert who specialized in this. The result was a highly successful surgery!

Strive for excellence on the most critical items. You will be rewarded.

Lesson 11
Focus

"The man who chases two rabbits, catches neither." —Confucius

The ability to focus is essential to winning in business and in life.

Unfortunately, many have lost this ability in today's fast-paced world with the proliferation of social media and instant communication tools.

Johann Hari chronicled this in his book *Stolen Focus—Why You Can't Pay Attention*. I highly recommend this book. Here are a few key tidbits:

- We touch our phones an average of 2,617 times in 24 hours.
- We are bombarded by 174 newspapers of material a day.
- Teenagers can focus on one task for only 65 seconds at a time, and office workers for only three minutes.

That is astonishing, and it is only getting worse. There is no way to effectively focus on the winning priorities with this constant interruption.

To fix this, you need to employ all the winning lessons but place high emphasis on Lessons 7–10: Prioritize, Simplify, Less is More, and 10/50. I also recommend that you provide "social media-free zones/times" to block out this constant interruption. Focus on one task at a time until it is complete.

One of the key benefits of focus is that it allows you to "get in the zone." The zone is something that is hard to describe, but you know when you are in it. You can tune everything else out, concentrate only on your primary task, and your performance significantly elevates. Many star athletes excel at doing this. I experienced this at work and at play. At work, when I am in the zone, I don't even hear anyone speaking to me, as my focus is total. Golf was one of my passions early in life. My peak performance was when I was a high school junior. I found the "zone" and was able to focus and visualize success. I went from the JV team to number 2 on our varsity golf team with my all-time best scores.

Sharpen your Focus. Get in the zone and stay there. Catch the rabbit.

Lesson 12
Align

"Unity is strength…
When there is teamwork and collaboration, great things can be achieved."
—Mattie Stepanek

Alignment of all resources, including people, is essential to success.

This is well understood in the military and in sports.
Winning teams preach and practice this.

I just finished a book (following my one-book-a-day approach) called *Boys in the Boat* that illustrates this well. It is about the gold-winning USA eight-man rowing team from the 1936 Olympics. For the boat to move as fast as possible, it requires all eight of the rowers to be aligned, pulling their oars in rhythm together. This is called "the swing." If one of the rowers' pace is not aligned, the boat will slow down, and they will not win. This is true even if one rower is pulling harder and faster than the others.

This is also true for other sports teams. If one member of the football or basketball team is playing a different defense (e.g., playing zone instead of man-to-man), someone will probably be left wide open. If this is done more than a few times, that team will have a hard time winning.

This same principle applies to business. If the business employees or financial resources are not aligned properly with the top priorities, then the likelihood of winning is materially lowered. This sounds easy to do in theory, but it is hard to do in practice. Too often, the squeaky wheel gets the grease. Too many resources are spent putting out fires instead of maintaining focus on the few critical business drivers.

Invest time to ensure alignment. Achieve great things.

Lesson 13
Define/Develop Clear Roles/Skill Sets

"If you don't define roles, people will define them for you."
—Danny Kerr

Identify what key skills are required to achieve your passion.

This should be a short list that is tailored to your unique situation. This is common practice for sports teams and important for your personal life.

Some examples will help illustrate this.

If you are putting together a winning basketball team, some key skills you need are accurate three-point shooters, great creators/scorers, and tough defenders. Remember to seek the top 10 percent of skills where possible.

If your personal passion is being a winning singer, a key skill you need is a great and/or unique voice.

The same concept applies to business. For instance, if your target market is direct to consumer, one required skill set would be great Internet sales and marketing capability.

Early in the company life cycle, only a few skill sets are needed and can be supplemented via your A+ Virtual Team (Lesson 23). This will grow over time with company size, but you can still follow the same approach.

Once the required skill sets are defined, roles also need to be clearly defined and delineated. Everyone should know their specific role and how that relates to their specific skill set. Avoid ambiguity and redundancy. Less is more.

Clearly define key skills and roles. Develop them. Achieve your passion.

Lesson 14
Instill Responsibility/Accountability

"The price of greatness is responsibility."
—Winston Churchill

There are many theories about the optimal organizational design. I have worked in a wide variety of them, with mixed results in each type.

The one essential element that is needed is to instill clear responsibility and accountability. There can be no guessing here. If everyone is responsible, then no one is responsible. Who has responsibility for each area should be easy for every stakeholder to understand, whether external or internal. Once responsibility is given, then accountability must follow.

Remember to simplify, use less is more, align, and define clear roles.

Most matrix organizations are good in theory but lousy in practice. They violate the lessons above and muddy the waters on responsibility and accountability. Stay away from them, where possible.

Again, sports teams understand this very well. A head coach has ultimate responsibility and accountability for team performance. The coach is rewarded if the team is successful and suffers the consequences if not.

Company CEOs usually have this as well (although not always, depending on their board's composition). The challenge is to have clear responsibility at all levels of the company. A particular emphasis needs to be placed on the key business units unique to that company. If it is a product-driven company, then the product business leader should ideally have responsibility and accountability for all the financial results. This includes the P&L and the balance sheet. Many companies go part of the way by tracking revenue and margin. Winning companies also include the full income statement and the balance sheet, which include the working and fixed investments required for that business.

Instill clear responsibility and accountability. Achieve greatness.

Lesson 15
Build Winning Values/Culture

"Try not to become a man of success, but a man of value."
—Albert Einstein

To create a winning team, build as many of the following winning values into your own culture as possible. This then becomes your culture.

1. **Authenticity/Trustworthiness**—Fake people lead to losing. And you can't fake true authenticity and trustworthiness. One of the companies I worked at held a three-day "authenticity" seminar. That is telling in itself. If you have to teach someone to appear to be authentic, you have a problem. The team can see right through that, as the leader's actual behavior gives them away. See Lesson 25 (Actions over Words). I left the company shortly after this.
2. **Integrity/Honesty**
3. **Dependability/Loyalty**
4. **Results-Oriented**
5. **Pride and Drive**
6. **Expectation/Visualization to Win**—Vince Lombardi was the master at this. He taught, "Winning isn't everything; it is the only thing."
7. **Competitiveness to Win**—Michael Jordan is a stellar example here. His sheer will to win, added to his skills, lifted the team to six titles.
8. **Team over Individual**—Tom Brady is a great example of this. In addition to his competitiveness to win, Brady was the ultimate team player who did what it took to win vs. padding individual stats or getting the most money.
9. **Dedication**
10. **Decisiveness**
11. **Persistence**
12. **Confidence/Positivity**—These traits are contagious.
13. **Solution-Focused:** Asks "How can we?" rather than "Why we can't?"
14. **Kindness**
15. **Learning passion and aptitude**

Chase perfection with your values and culture. Catch excellence.

Lesson 16
Hire/Retain/Promote/Reward Values Fit

"What we know matters, but who we are matters more."
—Brene Brown

Create a list of the required winning values for your company. This should start with the values listed in Lesson 15, but it needs to be tailored to your individual needs as no two companies are identical.

The best way to get winning values into your company is to hire them. Many of the winning traits are ingrained in individuals at an early age. Spend the critical time needed to fully vet this right from the start. Do as much due diligence as you can. Spend the time on proper reference checks and don't just rely on an interview—some people are exceptionally good at interviewing.

Even with the goal of hiring people with the key values, there will be some employees who do not have the right values. Identify them and make the necessary changes early.

Then develop and retain the key employees who do have the right value fit, as they are invaluable to your team.

And don't forget to promote and reward the key employees.
They will be worth it if you do and you may regret it if you don't.
More on this in Lesson 18 (Reward/Reinforce Desired Performance).

Once you do this consistently over time, you will create a winning culture and winning expectations in your business. This will last beyond the career span of some employees. This is what the dynasty sports teams have done.

Hire in, retain, promote, and reward values fit. Create the dynasty.

Lesson 17
Hire/Leverage/Align Strengths

"Don't let what you cannot do interfere with what you can do."
—John Wooden

In Lesson 13 (Define/Develop Clear Roles/Skill Sets), we focused on the key skills required for you to win.

The key to Lesson 17 is to focus on acquiring and leveraging the strengths of those skills, not on improving their weaknesses. More strength in the right key skills will help you win when combined together in a team. This combination increases power and effectiveness and leads to winning.

Again, sports teams know this very well. They do everything they can to find true stars in the most valuable skill-set positions (e.g., quarterback in the NFL). They then supplement that with key role players who excel in their skills. And crucially, they align the players together to perform as a team and tailor the plan to leverage their players' individual strengths.

Bobby Knight did this exceptionally with the 1976 Indiana basketball team, the last men's Division 1 team to finish undefeated at 32–0.

Bill Belichick was another master at this with the New England Patriots; he won six NFL championships despite not necessarily having the most individually talented teams.

Build and leverage your strengths and your business team's strengths. You will have a more successful and enjoyable life and business career.

Lesson 18
Reward/Reinforce Desired Performance

"Brains, like hearts, go where they are appreciated."
—Robert McNamara

To motivate your team and business to take the right actions to win, you need to properly reward and reinforce desired performance.

Make the reward lucrative and widespread, with short- and long-term incentives. You want it to be highly motivating. You want to pay it out. If done right, it is a win-win for all. You want the long-term incentives to be a retention tool—they need to be material and viewed as attainable. Successful private equity firms totally get this—they do it right.

Many larger, more established companies do not—they do it wrong. Often, large companies restrict the incentive pool to higher-level employees only; they are more focused on keeping the incentive pool low rather than getting the maximum benefit and payouts. And often they set incentives on the wrong metrics, ones that aren't aligned with the key winning priorities. As a result, the company does not win.

Ensure that you consistently apply rewards. Follow Lesson 25, "Actions Over Words." Employees will immediately notice if this is not done, particularly if the senior executives receive favorable treatment or if the wrong employees or behaviors are rewarded.

Align the incentives to the right metrics. They need to incorporate true EVA (Economic Value Added), not just a few income statement metrics. The further you go down to the P&L bottom line, the better. Using EBITDA (Earnings Before Interest, Taxes, Depreciation, Amortization—cash operating profit) is better yet. The best approach also takes the investment required to deliver the EBITDA into account.

Appreciate, reward, and reinforce the desired performance.
It will then continue.

Lesson 19
Set High Standards

"The greatest danger for most of us is not that our aim is too high and we miss it, but that it is too low and we reach it."

—Michelangelo

To win in life and business, set high standards. The higher the better.

It has been proven over and over again in numerous research studies that this works. Higher standards lead to higher performance. The inverse is also true: lower standards lead to lower performance.

As Vince Lombardi famously said, "Chase perfection, and you will catch excellence." That is exactly what he did.

My mother set very high standards and expectations for our entire family. My teachers and bosses set very high standards and expectations for me as well. But most importantly, I set very high standards for myself.

Set high standards for yourself. You will be surprised how far you can go.

I used this approach for this book. My expectations are for the book to meaningfully impact people's lives and careers and become a bestseller as a result. While I cannot control this outcome, I can control the quality and content of the book to make that possible. That is what I have done to the best of my ability.

Aim high. Aim very high. You will reach greater heights.

Lesson 20
Do Things Right

"If something is worth doing, it is worth doing right."
—Hunter S. Thompson

This is the expectation of all stakeholders and should be your own as well.

You cannot win if you do not do things right.

Think about your personal life. Would you go to a heart surgeon who got the heart surgery right about 50 percent of the time? How about a pilot who flew safely 90 percent of the time?

The same holds true for business. Your expectations of your suppliers are that they will deliver quality products on time in full quantity, 95 to 99 percent of the time. Your customers expect the same of you.

To help you do this, it is important to follow the other winning lessons. It is much easier to do things right with a simple business model of one product SKU (like Red Bull in the early years) than a highly complex business model of 1,000 different SKUs and 1,000 different customers.

This is why this lesson is number 20. Not that it is less important than the earlier ones; it is because you need to do all the earlier lessons to be able to effectively do things right.

Simplify, prioritize, focus. Take pride. Do things right. It is worth it.

Lesson 21
Employ Winning Habits

"We are what we repeatedly do. Excellence is not an act, but a habit."
—Aristotle

Most people have daily routines. Once established, they are hard to break.

That is why it is critical to build into your routine important steps toward your definition of winning and remove items that do not add value or are blockers to your success.

You can start small, but you need to repeat the behavior daily. Commit to the behaviors and to making the change. The closer that you can align them with your passion, the easier it will be for you to do so.

It is helpful if you get assistance from others. Use your tribe and virtual team. Publicly commit to your goals. Share your progress with your friends and colleagues. If possible, have some of your tribe join in on some of your activities. It will increase your likelihood of sticking with the activities, as it will add peer pressure. You will also have more fun.

My daily habits are pretty consistent and have been for much of my working life/career. I am an early-to-rise and early-to-bed guy. I use my early morning time to catch up on the world and plan my priority activities for the day. Exercise is one of my priorities; I ensure I carve out time for this—either first thing in the morning or as a midday break to reduce stress and jump-start the afternoon. I follow up on all priority messages/activities each day (basic follow-up skills are essential but are a lost art today). I close the day by putting everything in its rightful place (including all communications) and doing a "reset" so that tomorrow will be a fresh start. Having fun is mixed in as well.

While everyone is different, a rule of thumb is that it takes 21 days to form a habit and 90 days to make it permanent.

Commit to winning habits. Prosper.

Lesson 22
Use RFP

"If you can't fly then run, if you can't run then walk, if you can't walk then crawl, but whatever you do you must keep moving forward."
—Martin Luther King Jr.

RFP does not stand for request for proposal for this lesson.

RFP actually refers to Relentless Forward Progress on your top priorities.

I'll give a shout-out to my ultra-trail running friends for this term. Many of them run 50–100-mile trail runs. These are long, tough events that require strong mental and physical endurance and commitment. RFP refers to keeping moving forward, no matter how tough it is. Focus on getting to the next aid station or some other short-term goals. Continue doing this, and you will reach the finish line. The mental aspect of this is the most important thing.

The New England Patriots used this approach to claw their way back to a Super Bowl win after being down by 28–3. They couldn't make this deficit up all at once, but they could continuously chip away at it until the finish line was within reach.

RFP also applies very well to acquisitions. To get to the finish line, you need to keep momentum. Deals are fragile, and there are many moving variables (changes in your company, changes in the acquisition target, changes in the global economy, and so on). Once momentum is lost, it is often hard to restart.

The key is to use RFP for the right things, which are the agreed-upon top priorities in your life and business.

Keep moving forward; forward is a pace. Stay confident. Be persistent.

Lesson 23
Deploy an A+ Virtual Team

> *"Teamwork remains the most powerful competitive advantage because it is so powerful and so rare."*
> —Patrick Lencioni

The power of virtual teams is materially underused or underleveraged.

A virtual team means an extension of your formal organization (external) or reporting boundary (internal). It usually consists of specialists who excel in their roles when needed. Remember to find the top 10 percent.

Entrepreneurs starting a business understand how critical this is. Often, the entrepreneur is on their own or has only a few employees with limited capital. They need external assistance (advisors, suppliers, manufacturers, distributors, etc.) and truly value it at this stage.

This is also well understood by each of us in our personal lives. Our virtual team naturally consists of our friends, family, doctors, dentists, hairstylists, real estate brokers, plumbers/trade, and many other specialists in their roles.

As companies grow, many tend to lose focus on virtual teams and instead add employees too fast. This can result in violating Lessons 7 to 17. It's better to leverage virtual teams where you can, particularly for skills that are not required daily. Add employees slowly. Ensure you hire/align the right ones. Avoid bad partners – they can damage you as Boeing learned.

I have successfully used virtual teams internally and externally (including customers and competitors), and could not have won in my career without them. The key advice is to use less is more and the top 10 percent. Find the best specialist in the particular skill area you need. Ensure that the same virtual team member is consistently used for all matters when needed. They are an extension of your team and represent you to others. You will also build strong teamwork, camaraderie, loyalty, and alignment.

Unleash the hidden power of virtual teams. Capture the rare advantage.

Lesson 24
Cultivate Relationships

"Building relationships is not about transactions, it is about connections."
—Michele Tillis Lederman

Strong relationships are the glue needed to win in life and business.

Your family and core group of friends are essential to your happiness. To develop and maintain this core group, you need to invest quality time and effort. The rewards are clearly worth it.

One personal example is that I have maintained my grade school friendship and gotten together with my college freshman dorm friends every summer since 1982. This has taken a lot of commitment from all of us, but we have created lasting friendships and memories as a result.

The same is true in business. It truly is a small world, which is only getting smaller. Strong relationships are invaluable to help you get things done. You will need help both inside and outside your business. The world still revolves around relationships. Invest time in this. It will also make work and life much more enjoyable.

Strong relationships also help build trust in each other. Trust is essential. With trust, your team can create synergies, move faster, and excel.

Use the right communication methods at the right time. Text, email, and Zoom calls work as supplements, but they are not a replacement. They are not as personal as the real thing, and your message can be misunderstood. Relationships will be stronger if you also invest time in face-to-face meetings and old-fashioned phone calls.

Add the glue and make the investment to cultivate strong relationships.

Lesson 25
Actions Over Words

"You are what you do, not what you say you will do."
—Carl Jung

While your words are meaningful, they pale in comparison in significance to your actions.

Our society, particularly recently, has paid too much attention to words.

The problem with words is that it is often too easy to say what someone wants to hear.

The truly hard part is delivering the action behind the words.

We all know this in our personal lives. If a family member, friend, or service provider promises to do something but their behavior is different, we will clearly see and remember this. It can result in a loss of confidence and, potentially, a loss of trust.

The same is true in business. Company employees and stakeholders are pretty smart. They can see right through someone who does not back up their words with the promised actions and behaviors. You can't fake authenticity. Leaders can't implement policies or reward systems and then treat employees (or themselves) differently. It will get noticed and destroy your winning culture.

Contrast that with friends or leaders who back up their words with their actions. They gain your respect and loyalty.

Focus on taking the right actions. Deliver on your words. Be trusted.

Lesson 26
Silence Is Power

"The fool speaks, the wise man listens."
—Ethiopian Proverb

This is one of the most powerful negotiation lessons that I learned early in my business career and have applied throughout my life.

I was once on a business trip to Japan, exploring a potential acquisition. We had a meeting with a large group of around 20 people—half of them were from the Japanese target company, three were from our company, and the others were advisors and translators. As no one in our company spoke Japanese, we needed translators. It was a long, frustrating meeting.

We would speak and have it translated. The Japanese target employees would sit in silence and eventually say a few words to be translated back. This went on for hours and hours. Later that night at a karaoke bar (yes, the Japanese love this, and it is another great story in itself), I was told the real scoop by the Japanese team leader. It turned out that the entire Japanese team spoke fluent English. They used the translators because they didn't want us to know that they were listening to everything we said, including side conversations. They used it for effect and to gain time. They had also been saying few words in response. Finally, he left me with this thought: "Americans talk too much and listen too little. Silence is power. If we stay silent, it will drive Americans crazy. They will end up wanting to speak again and will negotiate against themselves."

The lesson and power of silence were made loud and clear to me.

Think about your personal situation when buying or selling a home. Waiting for the offer response can be agonizing. The most powerful and frustrating negotiating tactic is truly silence.

Use silence to your advantage.

Lesson 27
Remove Cancer Early

"You never know how toxic something is until you breathe fresher air."
—Unknown

This is an obvious lesson for our personal lives. Most people know that you want to remove any cancer as early as possible, as it gives you the best chance of winning against it and recovering. This is why it is recommended that you get annual physicals (Lesson 46), so you can diagnose cancer quickly.

We also know the phrase "one bad apple spoils the bunch." It's a simple phrase, but one that is not always followed in life and in business.

I have seen the negative effects of "cancer" with the sports and business teams that I have been part of. If one or a few individuals do not embrace the winning values (Lesson 15), they can bring the entire team down.

Sometimes this occurs with low performers. Often, the lowest performers do eventually get removed, but it happens too slowly. Remember Lesson 10, "10/50, 20/80, 30/90."

The bigger challenge is actually those individuals who are perceived to be high performers but who don't embrace the winning values. Often these individuals are chasing individual glory over team performance or worse. Companies are often reluctant to remove these individuals due to concern over short-term business results. Don't be reluctant. Remove them early. The problems with that individual will likely get worse over time and may metastasize across the company.

Remove cancer as quickly as possible and breathe the fresher air.

Lesson 28
Innovate

"There's a way to do it better—find it."

—Thomas Edison

Innovation is the true lifeblood of most companies (and individuals).

It is how most companies start. The early years are usually periods of intense innovation. Over time, the pace and impact of innovation slow down. Companies get complacent, particularly ones with a market lead. Companies also get too reliant on using acquisitions, which are often a highly expensive and risky crutch, to solve their organic growth problems. As a result, many well-established market-leading brands lose significant market share and even lose market leadership to start up entrepreneurial companies. The pace of this is accelerating in today's instantaneous and pervasive social media world.

I once had the opportunity to take a PhD class in marketing. I was the only non-PhD program student, and it gave me a great, differing perspective (Lesson 39). There was one very insightful takeaway in this class.

The key takeaway was that while innovation is crucial, it may not be enough just to innovate to win in the long term. Innovation can be copied over time, often at a lower cost. To win long-term, companies must also innovate to create path dependencies.

Path dependencies are a fancy term for product/service bundling. A historical example of this is the Beta vs. VHS video recording battle. Beta was the superior technology. VHS won by having the VHS product bundled with other products that were required for it to work. It was easier for the sellers and for the consumers, and that won out. Apple is a more recent example of a company that has brilliantly applied this. Once Apple gains a customer for one of their products, they create "path dependencies" for other Apple products, and soon their customers are buying all of them. It is difficult for a dependent customer to switch away.

Find the better way. Innovate and create path dependencies.

Lesson 29
Define the Root Issue

"When solving problems, dig at the roots and not at the leaves."
—Anthony J. D'Angelo

This is another lesson that sounds simple on its surface, but it is not.

Most recognize the importance of this when it comes to your health. If you have a major illness, you clearly want to find the root cause of the illness and not just treat the symptoms.

As I have learned, many doctors start by treating the more readily identifiable symptoms, usually with products from Big Pharma. They keep trying different "solutions" and try to rule things out in a way that is similar to Dr. House on the early 2000s TV show. The better approach is to spend a little more time to find the root cause, and then apply Lesson 10 to find the top 10 percent of doctors to fix it. That is what I did with my heart issue, with success. Moreover, I am taking no ongoing medication.

I learned the value of this lesson in my evening MBA class at the University of Minnesota. The class was solely dedicated to defining the root issue. At first, I thought this was crazy. We would do a case study and then write a 10-page paper on what the root problem at the company was. We never even addressed potential solutions. By the end of the class, I saw the light and became a convert. I have been preaching this ever since. You absolutely cannot develop the right solution unless you first truly define and understand the root problem. And often the problem is not the obvious area in which the symptoms are showing.

Businesses, governments, and people are too quick to try short-term fixes for symptoms instead of first understanding the true root issue and then committing the resources needed to actually fix it.

Be different. Dig at the roots and define the root issue. Win.

Lesson 30
Depth before Breadth

"Success demands singleness of purpose."
—Vince Lombardi

Building on your strong foundation rather than spreading out your resources seems like a rather simple concept, and it is simple. However, that doesn't mean that it is always adhered to.

The diversification phase was all the rage in the '70s. Companies acquired businesses that had no direct fit or strategic logic other than that they helped "diversify" the risk and provide additional growth opportunities. Common sense was not used here (see Lesson 36). To no one's great surprise, many of these moves failed spectacularly and had to be unwound at a great cost.

If an investor wants to diversify their holdings, they can do so via numerous investment index funds. They do not need a company or business to do this.

Remember Lessons 8, "Simplify," 9, "Less Is More," 11, "Focus," and 17, "Leverage and Align Strengths." Adding additional depth and strengths to the key drivers of your passion fortifies and better protects them.

The military knows this very well; it is one of the main lessons in military strategy. It is embodied in the "principle of force," which states you should keep resources concentrated. Germany famously violated this in WWII by fighting a major two front war, in the West against the Allies and in the East against Russia. This separated and depleted their resources, ensuring their eventual demise.

Use this lesson in your personal life as well. Build on your own "talent stack" to create a few "have-to-have" skills that are superior to others. Then you will be the ideal choice for someone else's virtual team.

Keep singleness of purpose and your resources concentrated. Succeed.

Lesson 31
Protect Core Profits

"There is only one boss, your customer."

—Sam Walton

Per Lesson 10, the top 10 percent of your products and customers typically generate around 50 percent of your profits. This is your core product and customer base.

Job 1 should be to protect your core profit base. Never take your eye off this ball. First, defend it so you don't lose it. Then focus your top priorities on growing it. It is much easier to build your core base, with which you have higher odds of success, than it is to branch out beyond this. Studies have shown that 80 percent of growth comes from core products. That doesn't mean you can't branch out, but if you do, be very mindful of what Job 1 is.

Many companies I have worked for and have observed have forgotten Job 1. They took their core base for granted. They shifted resources to new areas, or worse, to problem areas outside the 20/80 zone. Then slowly, their core base eroded, as did their profitability and growth.

This is particularly true with acquisitions. Acquisitions, when done right, can be extremely beneficial. When done wrong, they are harmful. One of the big dangers is that, given the large amount of resource effort required to integrate acquisitions, the focus is often taken off the core profits of both companies. As a result, both core bases erode. Be mindful here.

Remember Job 1. Always protect your core profits.

Lesson 32
Cash Is King

"Cash is king. Get every drop you can and hold onto it."
—Jack Welsh

Cash is the undisputed king.

This is something that is understood early in life by most of us.

It is extremely clear to many entrepreneurs who start their own businesses. They need money to start up their business and must closely watch their cash burn rate as they grow and expand. While margin percentages are important, you can't put accounting percentages in the bank.

For some reasons, this simple tenet gets lost for publicly held companies as they grow larger. (Private equity businesses keep their focus on cash.)

Large public companies place far too much emphasis on accounting metrics like quarterly EPS, which do not necessarily track key business performance. This can be detrimental, particularly if the company gets caught up in the quarterly EPS growth game.

Lesson 6, "Do the Right Things," already showed you its disastrous impact on one major historical food company that ceased to exist due to its obsession with quarterly EPS growth.

In another CPG company I worked for, they also played the quarterly EPS game at a high cost. Every quarter it got worse, and the company was offering large discounts to customers just to move up orders by a few weeks to make the accounting numbers. Huge resources were being spent on this instead of on projects growing the business. It was a bubble waiting to burst, which it eventually did, as all bubbles do.

Remember the king.

Lesson 33
Embrace Reality

*"Truth is not what you want it to be.
It is what it is, and you must bend to its power or live a lie."*

—Miyamoto Musashi

Reality cannot be ignored except at a price. The longer that you ignore it, the higher price you will pay.

To win in life and business, you have to understand the true state of where you are at all times. Fooling yourself to make yourself feel better does not lead to better results. Instead, it often takes you down the wrong path.

This needs to start with you. Use the mirror test—look in the mirror every day and be honest with yourself. Do you like what you see?

It works best when you surround yourself in life and in business with people who will tell you the reality, no matter how difficult it may be for you to hear in the short term.

Large companies are especially poor at this. There are too many layers and filters in place in organizations, so even if one layer provides reality, it does not make it all the way to the top. Many incentive systems are also poorly designed so that employees are actually rewarded or promoted to provide comforting lies instead of embracing reality. As a result, major issues are often hidden, but they eventually surface. They always do.

One of my brand traits is to be a reality provider. This was often embraced by people and businesses in my life. However, sometimes it wasn't. I had to make the hard choice to move on when I was not aligned with them. It did cause short-term pain, but it was the right long-term move to make.

Make the tough call to embrace reality. Know who you are.
You will be better off in the long run and can pass the mirror test.

Lesson 34
Openly Debate, Then Align

"In all debates let truth be thy aim, not victory."
—William Penn

To successfully embrace reality, you need to allow open debate on the issues and opportunities. You cannot have yes people who lead you into a the-emperor-has-no-clothes situation.

Promote healthy discussion. By healthy discussion, I mean discussing the merits of competing alternatives. Discuss the best- and worst-case scenarios. Discuss probabilities—what key assumptions have to occur, what would be needed for the best-case scenario to happen, and what risk mitigation steps can be taken to avoid the worst case. Get specialist opinions from your extended virtual team. Have key team members make recommendations on major decisions in person.

Then once the open debate is complete, let the leader who has the ultimate responsibility and accountability make the decision.

Once the decision is made, the full team needs to be supportive and aligned with it. This is true even if the team initially disagrees with the decision. The task for all is to do things right, as per Lesson 20.

If the results of that decision are not going as planned or desired, the team needs to embrace reality per Lesson 33 and communicate this upward. If corrective action is needed, then it can be done in a timely manner.

Let truth be your aim. Be victorious in the long run.

Lesson 35
Illusory Precision

*"The greatest obstacle to discovery is not ignorance—
it is the illusion of knowledge."*

—Daniel J. Boorstin

You are taught in school that there is only one correct answer, and you are given all the data you need to find the answer. Business and life do not work that way. You will have incomplete data and will need to make assumptions about future events to arrive at a decision.

Statistics can project confidence and be comforting when they support your position. Often, the more detailed they are, the more trusted they are.

This can lead to the problem of "illusory precision." False knowledge can be dangerous at worst and a large waste of resources either way.

Here is an example that illustrates this: When I joined a company as the head of planning, the historical annual budgeting process took nine months and significant resources to complete! This was not a good use of resources and violated upcoming Lessons 42 and 45. The primary driver of this was the process of setting the "standard cost" (used Lesson 29 to find the root cause).

The standard cost is a theoretical estimate of the product cost; it uses subjective allocations of overhead costs. There is no absolute right number; it is just an approximate estimate. However, that didn't stop the standard cost from being calculated to four decimal points! This created the illusion that it was absolutely correct. The process to do this took six months! We eliminated this step and reduced the budgeting timeline to three months. Good step, but there is a better approach per Lesson 45.

Instead of wasting resources on illusory precision, use the 20/80 rule.

Focus on the big picture and the critical assumptions and drivers. Remove the obstacle to discovery.

Lesson 36
Common Sense Wins

"Common sense is not so common."

—Voltaire

Use common sense to win.

It is a simple lesson, but it is not followed enough.

Sometimes, it is easier to rationalize a decision that you want to make than to embrace the reality that it is not the right decision.

Filter out the noise and propaganda trying to influence you. Leverage your experiences. Think. If it sounds too good to be true, then it likely is. Sometimes the experts will create a story to sell you a product/service.

One example of this comes from consultants and/or investment bankers. They can create a vision where your business will spend millions of dollars on their fees and advise your company to acquire another to broaden or diversify your profile. A wrong investment advisor will put together a fancy slide deck and sales pitch and say that if you do this, you will create significant synergies. If you are desperate for growth, you may believe them.

Before you sign the contract or wire money, check with your trusted tribe or virtual team. Get their valued opinions. The right virtual team advisor will put your interests first. Remember to embrace reality.

One simple step is to ask a few nonteam members if they understand the rationale and agree that it makes common sense. If they couldn't do so, it probably does not pass the sniff test and should be rethought.

Trust your real gut here.
It has been well trained for many years through many life experiences.

Lesson 37
Use All of Your Senses

"The five senses are the ministers of the soul."
—Leonardo da Vinci

Life is more enjoyable when you can experience all your senses.

Your body has been trained for this; the impact is magnified the more the senses (sight, sound, smell, taste, touch) are combined together.

It is easy to understand why businesses that capture all five senses together are highly successful. This should be your goal when possible.

High-end restaurants are masters at this. They deliver sight in a few ways: the visual atmosphere outside and inside the restaurant, the appearance of their entire staff, and the visual presentation of the food on their table. They deliver sound from the music they play to create an uplifting ambience. They deliver smells through the wonderful aromas of the food. They deliver taste by combining multiple subtle flavors. Finally, they deliver touch through the texture of the food dishes that they create. The combined effect is powerful, and it helps justify their hefty price tag.

Mallory combined a few senses to great effect to disrupt the battery category. They used sight by developing a new brand with a clear benefit description (Duracell) and by using two product colors to highlight the differentiated feature (copper top). They then used distinctive sounds (the three chimes) in their ads to reinforce the memory.

When I was at a food company, we had a fabulous R&D team. I have found this to be true at most businesses—they are an underappreciated and underused asset. The R&D team developed a pizza that combined all five senses into one product. It was a work of art and tasted great. Unfortunately, it never got to market as leaders were too focused on low-price targets rather than what the consumers truly wanted.

Unleash the ministers of your soul. Use all five senses when you can.

Lesson 38
Learn from History/Others

"Learning is a matter of gathering knowledge; wisdom is applying that knowledge."
—Dr. Roopleen

Many key lessons do not have to be reinvented. They can be observed by astutely studying history and other industries. There have been many iterations of trial and error over time. See what has failed and what has succeeded. Understand why. Determine if these lessons may apply to you or your business.

One example of this is the long-term trend toward premium craft products. Starbucks was one of the first to do this in coffee, with great success that disrupted the coffee industry. Premium craft beers followed this trend in the beer industry. As they were growing in popularity, I learned about an interesting confirmation of the 20/80 lesson. Liquor stores were only allocating 20 percent of their shelf space to craft beers (80 percent still went to the mass-produced beers), but craft beers provided 80 percent of the liquor store's beer margins as they were higher-priced with higher margins. Liquor store owners noticed this and started allocating more shelf space to craft beers.

Going back to the pizza story from the last lesson, the company I worked for had observed the success of craft beer. We thought that the craft trend could also apply to the pizza industry. We saw that the fastest-growing frozen pizza brands were regional, specialty, high-priced pizzas. These brands had a relatively small customer base with limited distribution, but the trend was unmistakable. Our R&D team developed a fantastic premium, craft frozen pizza. We had even acquired the rights to a super-premium brand to use for it. Unfortunately, we had a leadership change that shifted the corporate priorities, and it did not come to market. It was a missed opportunity.

Military and sports are two great areas to learn key winning lessons from.

There are numerous books on military and sports lessons. I recommend reading many of them if you can.

My two favorites are *The Art of War* by Sun Tzu and *Marketing Warfare* by Al Ries and Jack Trout.

Here are some specific lessons that the two recommended books (*The Art of War* and *Marketing Warfare*) include, along with some others:

Win the battle before it is fought (plan ahead, pick/tilt playing field in your favor)
Unity is the key driver of success (align)
Know thyself (embrace reality)
Maintain flexibility and adapt to changing circumstances
Use deception to hide your true intentions
Leverage forces and talent
- Keep your resources concentrated; launch an attack on as narrow a front as possible
- Use alliances to increase actual or perceived resources

Defense has a superior position if forces are close in strength
- An entrenched position is hard to overcome head-on
- Flank the enemy; Germany did this in WWII and went around the Maginot line

Speed and agility can beat size
- Football teams spread the field to leverage speed advantages

Keep something in reserve
- Be prepared for counterattacks and resource attrition
- One of the firms I worked at had no debt covenant reserve; it went bankrupt

Pursuit is key (you need to stay aggressive when you have the advantage)
Find the "Achilles' heel" of the opponent (one that is hard to change)
Understand your own "Achilles heel" (your worst fear) **and protect it**
Fully develop and leverage your unique resource strengths
Only the leader should focus on defense first
The best defensive strategy is the courage to attack yourself
Strong competitive moves should always be blocked
Understand competitor capabilities and prepare for attacks (play chess)
On-the-ground intelligence from the front is essential

Use your learning from history and others. Gain and apply wisdom.

Lesson 39
Understand Many Perspectives

"A shift in perspective opens a new set of unlimited possibilities."
—Satsuki Shibuya

When assessing major decision points in your own life or business, it is helpful to understand as many perspectives as possible before committing.

- Use your trusted, extended virtual team.
- Seek input from all your key stakeholders.
- Ensure you have diversity of thought.
- Include some on each side of the potential decision.
- Embrace reality.
- Make your major decision and commit to it.

Here is a story from my career where my perspective changed.

When I was at a family firm, they gave me the opportunity to lead the original equipment manufacturer battery business. It was my first line role after working in corporate for most of my career. It was quite an eye-opener, having direct in-person discussions with our key customers. This was especially true when our company had quality problems that affected the quality of their products and when we needed to increase prices materially. I quickly learned how this impacted their consumers and their business. Once I understood this, we were mutually able to work together to find solutions that worked for all. This opened my eyes to a different perspective, and I never forgot it.

Shift your perspective. Open up the unlimited possibilities.

Lesson 40
Engage Your Stakeholders

"Unengaged sponsor sinks the ship."
—Angela Waner

You have many stakeholders in your life and business.

In life, you have your family, friends, neighbors, organizations, community, advisors, virtual team, and others.

In business, you have your investors, shareholders, employees, suppliers, manufacturers, distributors, customers, consumers, advisors, financiers, virtual team, and others.

Remember Lesson 24 and cultivate relationships with your key stakeholders. Your stakeholders have a wealth of knowledge, experience, and connections. They can be a great asset to you if you heed their advice. This will be beneficial for all and will make life more enjoyable.

It is also important to maintain a proper balance among all key stakeholders. Sure, some of them are more important to you; they will and should have higher priority. But if you upset the balance too much by ignoring the impact on certain stakeholders, then you run the risk of not having their support when a critical issue arises. For most of us, there will be critical issues. That is life.

Engage your sponsors. Keep your ship afloat.

Lesson 41
Coach/Teach, Don't Manage

"A good coach can change a game. A great coach can change a life."
—John Wooden

To get the best out of your employees and teams, it is better to follow what many successful sports teams do than what many companies do.

Companies traditionally "manage" their employees. Employees are often placed or promoted into structured roles that do not match or optimize their capabilities. They are given rote tasks with deadlines. Policies are set on what employees can and cannot do. Companies watch over employees and point out mistakes. Annual performance appraisals provide a permanent record of what was done right and what needs improvement. The entire process is not pleasant, particularly if you are the one being managed. This does not lead to improved, optimum performance, and it does not lead to winning.

Sports teams assign position coaches to develop their players and optimize their units' and team's skills and performance. The best teams hire position coaches who are experts in their specialty and are good teachers. They identify, improve, and leverage the players' unique skill sets in the right roles. When done well, the process produces better results. Not to say that the position coaches don't have conflict with the players from time to time. Of course, they do. The key is balance. If it is balanced and constructive, the process is much more pleasant and productive.

Parents know this as well. The most effective teach their kids about life, how to think and make decisions, and embed values that will stay with them. The best guide their children but don't micromanage every activity.

Be a great coach. You may change a life and create better, happier results.

Lesson 42
Minimize Inward Activity

"Vision looks outward and becomes aspiration."
—Stephen S. Wise

To win, your resources and activities should be primarily focused externally on your customers and consumers. Follow Lesson 10. About 80 percent of your resources (in terms of dollars and people) should be focused on external stakeholders.

Unfortunately for many companies, the opposite is true, particularly for larger organizations. It seems that the larger the company, the greater the resource time spent on inward administrative activities. Many of them spend up to 80 percent of their time looking inward. If you work for a company like this, you know how frustrating this is. It seems most of your day is spent in internal meetings, replying to internal emails, and creating presentations for future internal meetings. This does not add value or help you or your company win.

This bureaucracy is sometimes called Parkinson's law. It is like lighter fluid for bureaucracy. This is the idea that work will generally expand to fill the amount of time, budget, and people allocated to it.

It's a business tapeworm that slowly eats away at companies, making them less and less efficient and innovative over time.

Minimize inward activity wherever possible.

Actively track the amount of time spent internally vs. externally.

Repeatedly ask, "How does this activity help my customer or consumer?" and "How does this help me achieve my key value drivers to win?"

Less inward activity is more.
Cast your vision outward. Achieve your aspiration.

Lesson 43
Minimize Presentations

"People who know what they are talking about don't need PowerPoint."
—Steve Jobs

One of the major drains on employee time are internal presentations.

They take a significant amount of time and effort at multiple levels of the organization. They also result in a large number of meetings, reviewing the various iterations prior to the ultimate meeting.

And worse yet, they take precious time away from the important business topics in the meeting. Discussion and debate of the key points end up being limited when this should be the primary focus of the meeting.

To solve this, companies need to actively limit the use of internal presentations. Save them for when they are truly needed.

For the needed presentations, require that they be sent out as a pre-read. Focus the meeting on discussion of the key issues and solutions. Do not begin the meeting by presenting the deck that was sent out. Reduce the number of pre-meetings as well. That is what the meeting itself is for.

I saw one highly effective example of this at a CPG company I worked for. One of our business leaders had a novel and creative approach to our board of directors' meetings. Previously, like almost all BOD meetings, there had been a large number of formal presentations that required a significant amount of work. The BOD meeting primarily went through this material. The business leader eliminated all the board presentations. Instead, he just spoke directly to the BOD and candidly discussed any topic or questions that they had. The BOD loved this approach, and the meeting itself was much more effective.

Minimize presentations. Use time saved on what matters, the customers.

Lesson 44
Walking around Works

"In every walk...one receives more than he seeks."
—John Muir

You have heard the phrase "management by walking around." This works.

It makes common sense. But why isn't it done more often?

When you "walk around" the office, you will informally meet up with many other employees and leaders. This leads to frequent, short, informal conversations about life and business. It cultivates relationships. It minimizes the need for formal meetings and presentations. It speeds up the decision-making process. It is enjoyable.

Unfortunately, the current trend is to do less of this and more communication via Zoom calls. This does not work as well.

One of the CPG companies I work for relocated their headquarters to Atlanta, Georgia. Initially, there were only seven of us in the office. While there were clearly some negatives about this move (the primary one was being disconnected from most of the USA business), there was one major positive. Since the seven of us were in such close proximity, we had numerous, frequent, short daily discussions. This was the walk-around method on steroids. And it worked well. Eventually, the small remote HQ office was disbanded and returned to the original USA location, but a winning lesson was learned.

If you work remotely, schedule recurring visits that maximize your time to informally meet up with as many colleagues as you can.

Invest the time to do walk-arounds.
You will reap the rewards and receive more joy along the way.

Lesson 45
No Annual Budget

"Waste neither time nor money, but make best use of both."
—Benjamin Franklin

One of the major inward-facing activities that consumes significant resources and time is the annual budget. The benefit of this process is not worth the resources. In fact, I believe it actually has a negative impact.

The stated objective of the annual budgeting process is to set a benchmark financial goal for the company, for the business unit, and for the key functional areas. Actual results are measured against it and used for evaluating and rewarding performance as part of the incentive plans.

The budget is an example of illusory precision as it is a highly subjective negotiated number. It is going to be wrong, as it is an estimate. Yet many months and dollars are spent on the process. The business wants the lowest target possible, so they "sandbag" their initial projections. Top management wants the highest target possible, so they push for unrealistic growth goals. The end result is often a negotiated compromise that no one is happy with.

It can be highly demotivating if bonuses are not achieved. It can also lead to gamesmanship to achieve a bonus by doing activities that do not support the key value drivers.

I have worked for a variety of businesses. Some made this process work okay. Many did not. Some had a highly demotivating impact. Budgets often end up being set from the top down with high, unattainable targets. The businesses actually performed well, but not at the high budget targets. As a result, the annual and long-term bonuses paid were nominal, resulting in poor employee morale and high employee turnover.

So what is the solution? *Eliminate the annual budget.* Base incentives on actual year-to-year and long-term goals performance. This removes the negotiation game and makes the best use of your time and money.

Lesson 46
Take Annual Physical

"It is health that is the real wealth, not pieces of gold or silver."
—Mahatma Gandhi

Most people know that they should have an annual physical examination done, particularly as they age. Blood tests can be very early indicators of potential health issues that are better addressed as early as possible. Even with this knowledge, many still choose not to do so.

I was one of those individuals. I did go every few years, but it was not an annual visit as I was feeling okay. Fortunately for me, I did at least go for a colonoscopy exam. While that particular exam came back benign, it was discovered that I had atrial fibrillation (an irregular heartbeat). I was able to catch it early and had ablation surgery to correct it.

The same annual physical examination should be done for businesses. Take this time to check in with all key stakeholders in person to see how you are doing. It is also wise to have an external specialist do an independent, unbiased review. Get their candid feedback on what is going well, what can be improved, and what is missing from what you really want or need. This will give you valuable information and help deepen your relationships, but only if you truly listen and act on their input. Embrace the reality. It may not be what you want to hear, but it is probably what you need to hear. And you will get the information early enough to make a difference.

Capture the real wealth. Take the annual physical.

Lesson 47
Do Scenario/Contingency Planning

*"To not prepare is the greatest of crimes;
to be prepared beforehand for any contingency is the greatest of virtues."*
—Sun Tzu

Military special forces spend a significant amount of their time doing scenario/contingency planning and dry runs of their plans before their missions. They do this because of the importance of their mission and so that they are prepared ahead of time to react quickly if issues arise.

This process works and is well worth the time invested.

Individuals and businesses should follow this wise approach for themselves when facing a major decision or event. Don't use it for day-to-day items. Do use it for the high-impact ones like acquisitions, major new product launches, job relocations, and others.

Identify the worst-case scenario. Identify probable competitive moves. Assess likelihoods. Develop mitigation plans and countermoves.

Use the scientific process: define the problem, gather background information, form a hypothesis, make observations, run quick experiments to test the hypothesis, and draw conclusions. Repeat as necessary.

When facing complex multiple-option scenarios, simplify it by comparing individual options against each other to narrow down the choices needed.

Once you do this, you will proceed with more confidence and will be able to react quicker and with more success when issues or opportunities arise.

*Prepare beforehand for material contingencies.
Gain the greatest of virtues.*

Lesson 48
Play Chess

*"To win you must first understand the endgame…
Every move must have a purpose."*
—José Raúl Capablanca and Bruce Pandolfini

Life and business are not simple games of checkers. They are more complex.

Chess is a good analogy for both life and business, as it is a game of strategy. It requires you to think numerous moves ahead, assess competitive game plans and possible future moves, and develop a counterplan for each potential strategy.

Too many people, businesses, and governments play checkers. They react emotionally to the next visible move ahead of them rather than being patient, rational, and strategic. Often, the result does not end well and leads to regret.

Evaluate and consider before making a major move. Understand and assess your opponent's incentives and end goals. Don't rush. Don't let your desire to win influence the move you make. Play the long game.

Chess is much more work than checkers. The game is more difficult to learn and master. The game itself is longer. Nonetheless, it needs to be learned and played to be able to win. Make it a priority and become better at playing it.

Understand the endgame. Make every move with a purpose. Prosper.

Lesson 49
Celebrate True Wins

"We do not remember days, we remember moments."
—Cesare Pavese

Life is too short and too hard not to enjoy it every chance you have.

You should take the time to celebrate the true wins in your life—the ones that are the most meaningful to you. Smaller wins can still be celebrated, but save the truly special celebrations for the ones that really matter. You will remember those memories later in life.

The same is true in business. Have a major celebration for the special true wins. Focus on your major business wins and outstanding individual performances that contribute to those wins. You want each individual to be emotionally connected to the business. Try to create the pride and joy that winning sports teams feel in their locker rooms after big games.

However, don't overdo this by frequently "celebrating" small, internally focused activities. This waters down the true wins and shifts the lens toward internal administrative activity rather than external business drivers and customers.

One special celebration that I will never forget was after the acquisition of a German consumer products company. It had been a long and challenging process. We celebrated the deal signing in a German castle. We had a formal signing ceremony and private party in the castle with both companies' leadership. At this castle event, our COO clinked my wine glass and said, "Jim, you just changed the history of the company." It is something I will never forget, and it still makes me proud even today.

Celebrate true wins. You will remember the moments for a lifetime.

Lesson 50
Use One-Page Summaries

"If you can't summarize an issue on one-page, you don't know understand the issue well enough."
—Ronald Reagan

The power of one-page summaries is a lesson I learned from a visionary boss in my early work in strategic planning at a major food company.

Encapsulating all your key thoughts on a subject into a one-page document is very hard to do. It forces you to identify the most critical elements, discard the less essential ones, assign top priorities, identify necessary trade-offs, and importantly decide what you are not going to do.

The benefits of doing this are worth the effort. It helps you follow many of the winning lessons: identify key drivers, do the right things, prioritize, simplify, less is more, 10/50, focus, align, and do things right.

Unfortunately, many companies continue to use huge presentation decks with high complexity and high resource use (internal time and major consulting fees). These are often hard to understand, don't provide the strategic resource clarity required, and gather dust on a shelf/computer.

One of the large global companies I worked for implemented a new strategic planning process. I am actually a big fan of their process concepts. However, they did so by hiring a major consulting firm that tried to get every detail theoretically correct. This resulted in a hefty upfront price tag and a long, drawn-out planning process. The planning instruction manual itself was over 300 pages long! This did not work and wasted resources. Don't do this.

Take Ronald Reagan's advice and use one-page summaries.

Bonus Lesson 1
Don't Cheat on the Expense Report

> *"Cheating is a choice, not a mistake.*
> *Loyalty is a responsibility, not a choice."*
>
> —Unknown

This lesson dates back to the first summer of my career. I was an internal auditor at a major global company. One of the simple early assignments was to review a small sample of expense reports for our external auditors.

It was boring work. That was until I discovered "the expense report."

The report was from the top sales employee for a business unit. It had a few obvious minor items that overstated the expenses by around $1,000. I reviewed the report with his boss to see what he wanted to do, if anything.

Upon review, the boss quickly noticed that the sales employee should not even have been at some of the locations on this trip. He asked me to follow up on each expense item. That is where the fun started…

I started making calls, and here is what I found.

This top sales rep, who was married with two kids, had mistresses in multiple cities across the USA. And the city locations visited were not work destinations, but they were very close to US military installations.

At this point, I was pulled off the project, and it eventually went to US government authorities. It turned out that this guy was a spy. He was a military reserve pilot for a European country, had suspiciously ditched a fighter plane just off the coast of a Middle Eastern country, and was suspected of spying on US military bases. Soon thereafter, he was divorced and deported.

So *don't cheat on your expense reports! And be wary of those who do.* All this for $1,000!

Bonus Lesson 2
Set Tiered Goals

"Always remember, your focus determines your reality."
—George Lucas

To achieve your definition of winning, set tiered goals.

First, set a long-term goal for your personal life and career. It should be a high standard, tough to achieve, but attainable through persistent focus.

Next, set a midterm or interim milestone goal. This will give you something tangible to shoot for and allow you to celebrate a true win.

Then set a short-term goal that will be your day-to-day focus. This will help you make consistent progress toward your midterm and long-term goals. The short-term goal will change/evolve as you progress.

Remember to use RFP (Lesson 22) toward your goals.

My new personal long-term goal is to improve my fitness and health so I can be active and do major hiking/biking events. A few of my long-term event goals are to hike the Grand Canyon rim to rim and to hike and bike up to Mt. Lemmon in Tucson. These are highly strenuous activities, but they are attainable with proper training and focus.

The midterm milestone is to hike the Grand Canyon down to the river and back on the same day. Bonnie and I did this back in 1998, when we were much younger and had better fitness. This time, we want to hike it without having to walk on slippery ice with strong winds at the top!

My short-term goal is to rehab my shoulder and related injuries so I can hike simple, short, five-mile trails and overcome my fear of falling on the bike and reinjuring myself. My physical therapist is helping with this step.

Determine your reality. Set and focus on tiered goals.

Bonus Lesson 3
Speed Wins

*"Speed is the ultimate weapon in business.
All else being equal, the fastest company in any market will win."*
—Dave Girouard

Fast does win and saves money. Slow loses and burns money.

Key is to increase your speed while not sacrificing your quality.

The importance of this was imprinted on me during our lengthy and costly house builds and reinforced in publishing this book, which is why it is a bonus lesson added late in the process.

The value of speed is highly evident in sports. It is also highly beneficial in business and life.

The speed is often inversely related to the size of the organization. A single entrepreneur can move rapidly. A large, complex, multi-layered, bureaucratic organization often moves slowly. Decisions require multiple approval layers with each layer adding delays. Many steps are done sequentially with each individual delay having a ripple time and cost impact on future steps.

Many tactics can accelerate pace and have been discussed in prior winning lessons: Prioritize, Simplify, Less is More, Top 10%, Focus, Align, Instill Accountability/Responsibility, Reward Desired Performance, Set High Standards, Do Things Right, Deploy A+ Virtual Team, and others. Additional tools include critical path management, parallel processing, frequent iterations with short feedback cycles, and contingency planning.

Increase your speed and create the ultimate weapon.
Follow the winning lessons and remove the pace slowing barriers.

Bonus Lesson 4
Sometimes the Best Decisions Are Ones Not Made

"The quality of your life depends on the quality of your decisions."
—Ray Dalio

I shared a few stories of less favorable deals that the company would have been better off not making. Some of them were almost fatal.

There were numerous other bad deals that we successfully avoided by following the winning lessons. One deal was on the historical M&A target priority list. When it finally came up for sale, everyone was excited, until they weren't. Once we had a look under the hood, we learned that it wasn't as attractive as we thought. It could work, but only at the right value. We embraced reality and stayed disciplined. Our bid did not even advance us to the second round. The "winner" paid double what we bid. The deal was a very poor one for them and lost them a lot of value.

This lesson has even more meaning in your personal life. You will have several life-changing decisions and crossroads. Follow the lessons.

The first major decision for me was my college choice. I had a plan. I was focused on getting an undergraduate degree in accounting, as it was a great base to have. I had won a scholarship in this field. I researched schools that specialized in this (using the 10/50 rule). There were two in state schools, Whitewater (WW) and Eau Claire (EC), that were clearly superior to the others. Whitewater was traditionally ranked higher and was recommended to me by my teachers. EC had recently caught up and was at least on par, if not now ahead of WW. I was leaning toward EC. When I visited to check it out, I fell in love with the campus and knew it was the right choice for me.

A few other opportunities came up after my EC visit. I was offered a full scholarship to West Point. This is very hard to get and quite an honor.

I was also accepted into a few other major universities across the USA, including USC. It was quite heady for a teenager growing up in the small town of Green Bay, Wisconsin.

After much reflection, I decided to pass on these highly attractive options and stay with my earlier decision to attend EC. It was the right decision for me. I met lifelong friends and had great, caring teachers with small classes, a great academic experience, and a fabulous life experience.

The next key decisions were career-related. The "thing to do" for accounting grads was to get a job with the big 8 accounting firms if at all possible. It was pushed hard by all of the EC professors and counselors. I received an offer from PwC (one of the top eight firms). I turned it down and instead went to work for a global manufacturing firm in Minnesota. I liked their technology innovation focus and wanted a broader base. The job opened my mind to broad strategic thinking at an early age.

The easy thing for me to do was to stay at this firm and become a lifer. They were a great, well-respected company. Then an opportunity arose with a historic food company crosstown. They were extremely well respected in the finance area in particular. I also wanted to get my evening MBA, and their location was close to the campus. I took the leap.

My first few years at the company did not go exactly as planned. It started well, but then they had a reorganization (which happens a lot at larger companies, so look for the opportunities that arise). I had second thoughts about my decision to leave the global manufacturing firm and was considering returning. Then a job working on the corporate strategic financial plan opened up. There was little interest from applicants, as most of the time was spent preparing boring financial models. I viewed it differently as an opportunity. Moving to corporate strategy was a game changer for me. I quickly simplified the financial planning process by following the winning lessons and freeing up nine months of the year. This allowed me to work on actual strategic planning and assessing the corporate business portfolio. See Lesson 6 for more on this.

I later took a road trip down to Madison, Wisconsin, to go to a basketball game. I loved the atmosphere and vibe of the town, campus, and historic basketball arena. At halftime, by chance, I ran into my old college roommate. He told me a planning job was opening at his former company, a small CPG family firm, and that I should give the leader there a call. I did, and I set up an interview. Quickly, I met him and a few other key leaders. Immediately, I hit it off with them and knew they were aligned with my values per Lesson 15.

At the same time, I was approached by a recruiter for jobs at PepsiCo and Pizza Hut. PepsiCo was regarded as the top company in the USA for finance careers. I was fortunate to receive offers from both of them, along with an offer from the family CPG firm. The PepsiCo and Pizza Hut offers were much more financially lucrative. I even received a call from the CFO of PepsiCo to try to close the deal.

I went against conventional wisdom and joined the small CPG family firm. I am so glad I didn't make the decision to join the others. It was absolutely the right call for me. I ended up investing 21 years of my life there. It was a fabulous ride. In addition to the meaningful and fulfilling work experience, it allowed me to make numerous lifelong friends and have a fabulous life experience.

I won't go through all of the rest of the career stories, but the pattern continued. I passed on a decision to go to a more lucrative Wall Street career in NYC per Lesson 2, "Define Winning." I left firms when our values were no longer aligned. I joined a global food company late in my career after an interview process that mirrored my earlier family CPG experience. A recruiter called me and told me the hiring global M&A leader was visiting from Europe but was flying back from Chicago the next day. I seized the opportunity and flew to Chicago to meet him in person before his flight. I then met the key leadership team that week, immediately connected with them, and was hired.

But I will close with a more important personal story.

September 1996 was the most important, fateful time/decision in my life.

I am a major Wisconsin Badger football fan and attended a game with 18 of my friends. It was a five-star picture postcard day. The Badgers won, and the post-game tailgating was rocking. I was having a great time with my friends after the game, but I remembered that I had committed to attending a volleyball teammate's housewarming party. No one else wanted to leave the outdoor tailgate, but I needed to keep my word. I left the tailgate and went to the party by myself.

When I parked my car, I noticed this stunning blonde with a great smile in the driveway. I said to myself, *Who is this?* At the party, I was trying to find an opportunity to meet this woman one-on-one. Eventually, I was able to, and we had a clear connection. I invited her to a party I was hosting the next weekend.

Great news. She came to the party. When she walked in, I turned to a friend of mine and said, "That is the woman I am going to marry." I knew it immediately. Shortly thereafter, Bonnie and I went to a friend's lake cabin (affectionately named the "stabbin' cabin" by Bonnie's sister Sue, who thought this unknown guy could be an axe murderer—thanks Bart and Carol for the cabin invite). That trip further accelerated our relationship. We were on a fast track. We got engaged the following summer in Colorado (another great story) and married the next spring in Arizona.

I had found my soulmate and have been happily married for over 25 years.

So sometimes the best decisions are the ones you don't make.

Choose wisely.

Closing

"The wise man is one who knows what he does not know." —Lao Tzu
"The art of knowledge is knowing what to ignore." —Rumi

I hope you enjoyed reading this book and were able to have a few "aha" moments that will spark you to have a more enjoyable and successful life and career; however, this is defined by you.

While this book contains many lessons, stories, and frameworks, I encourage you to follow the 10 lessons below at a minimum for the greatest impact:

- *Commit to your passion*
- *Define winning*
- *Clarify your target market/brand*
- *Identify your key drivers*
- *Do the right things*
- *Prioritize and simplify*
- *Focus*
- *Do things right*
- *Cultivate relationships*
- *Celebrate true wins*

Know what you don't know. Know what to ignore.
Follow the winning lessons.

"Good luck; we are all counting on you" (one of favorite lines from *Airplane!*).

About the Author

Jim Kimble is the founder and chair of Aerie Strategy Group, LLC.

He is a leader in strategic management and corporate development, with 40 years of broad global business line and staff experience.

Jim has significant accomplishments in strategic planning, corporate development, business unit management, innovation, sales, investment management, financial analysis, and consulting in the consumer products, food, business-to-business, and hospitality industries.

He pioneered an innovative integrated strategic management system that focused company resources on critical core priorities to accelerate strategic profitable growth, increase ROI, and minimize risk.

Jim transformed the portfolio mix at two companies: increased net sales by seven times, EBITDA by 11 times, and enterprise value by 12 times at a CPG firm and doubled the ROI at a food business.

He led or created 72 strategic corporate development deals/opportunities: 14 deals that led to a 12x enterprise value increase at a CPG firm, 30 transactions with a value of over $3 billion at a food firm, and 28 high-impact opportunities at another business.

Jim currently resides in Arizona with his wife Bonnie and their two ragdoll cats. They enjoy experiencing the beautiful Southwest.